My life's work has  **the forgotten art o**̶ **nication and the po**̶**̶ that the right words at the right time can have to achieve the right results.**

Quite often the decision between a customer choosing you over someone like you depends on your ability to know exactly what to say, when to say it and how to make it count.

This book delivers tactical insight into the power of words and provides tools to empower success-driven individuals to get more of what they want.

If you are looking for more copies of this book for your team, contact speaking@philmjones.com and learn your options for bulk pricing and customization.

Abracadabra—you are a millionaire! That is what will happen if you follow the advice from Phil Jones in this book. Read it more than once and it means even more!

Jeffrey Hayzlett, primetime TV and podcast host, chairman of C-Suite Network

Indeed, the right words spoken the right way, while perhaps not actually magic, can sure have the results of such. Great job by the author in bringing us this very helpful guide.

Bob Burg, co-author of *The Go-Giver*

I think Phil says it best himself at the end of this fabulous read: "Everything you have learned in this book is simple, easy to do and works." It's tried and tested, proven and guaranteed to help you get your own way more often.

Philip Hesketh, professional speaker and author on the psychology of persuasion and influence

If you want to get prospects, clients, colleagues, bosses or anybody to say "yes" to what you want, I have three magic words of advice for you: "Get this book!" *Exactly What to Say* is a must-read for everyone who sells a product, a service or a story or wants to impress, motivate, engage and influence others from the very first moment. It will help you to use the most compelling phrases, to ask the right questions at the right moment, and to eliminate the wrong words from your personal and professional vocabulary.

Sylvie di Giusto, keynote speaker and corporate image consultant

This book is packed with ideas and easy-to-implement suggestions that will assist any individual in obtaining the outcomes they require from the conversations they have.

Grant Leboff, CEO, StickyMarketing.com

Implementing Phil's simple yet powerful Magic Words has been integral to the growth of our now–£20 million business over the last few years. In *Exactly What to Say*, Phil has delivered a book packed full of real-world solutions that will lead you to achieving the outcomes you desire in life and business.

Richard Dixon, director, Holidaysplease

The worst time to think of the best thing to say is always when you're actually saying it! I've long been a lover and student of great power scripts, killer questions and magical phrases that open doors and close sales. And there's nobody better than Phil Jones at finding that perfect key that will unlock a range of situations. If you want to sell more and influence better and take much less time doing it, then this book is as close as you'll get to a magic wand or silver bullet to success!

Rob Brown, founder of the Networking Coaching Academy and bestselling author of *Build Your Reputation*

Phil Jones helps uncover the truth in complex selling situations. These powerful phrases demonstrate how to influence others with integrity while never seeming pushy. You'll use these gems each and every day.

Ian Altman, co-author of *Same Side Selling*, Forbes.com columnist

If you want to be more influential in every situation, you need to master the simple yet powerful lessons contained within. *Exactly What to Say* could replace just about every other book on human behavior—it's that useful.

John Jantsch, author of *Duct Tape Marketing*

....

Have you ever considered why a horse can win a race and get ten times the earnings? Was the winner ten times better than the second-place horse? Hardly; she only won by a nose. The same applies to sales and marketing. What makes the winner a winner is a concept called "the winning edge." One of my early mentors drilled it into me that "everything you do either enhances or detracts from your ability to close the sale. No detail, however minute, is neutral." This is why I love Phil Jones's book *Exactly What to Say*. In this short but power-packed book, he shares how to use certain key phrases to help you with the winning edge. There is no doubt words matter a great deal in any marketing and sales situation, so make sure you have your Magic Words.

Bryan Eisenberg, *New York Times* bestselling author of *Waiting for Your Cat to Bark?* and *Be Like Amazon*

....

Exactly What to Say is a masterclass in the art of influence, persuasion and generating top-producing business results. This is a must-read for anyone looking to be more persuasive in their business and personal lives.

Seth Price, bestselling author of *The Road to Recognition*

EXACTLY
WHAT
TO SAY

EXACTLY

Phil M Jones

The Magic Words
for Influence
and Impact

WHAT TO
SAY

BOX OF
TRICKS

Box of Tricks
Hoboken, NJ
www.philmjones.com

ISBN 978-0-692-88195-8 (paperback)
ISBN 978-0-692-88196-5 (ebook)

Produced by Page Two
www.pagetwostrategies.com
Editing by Jenny Govier
Cover and text design by Peter Cocking

17 18 19 20 21   5 4 3 2 1

The worst time to think about the thing you are going to say is in the moment you are saying it. This book prepares you for nearly every known eventuality and provides you with a fair advantage in almost every conversation.

Opening Words

I am guessing that you picked this book up for one of a number of reasons.

Perhaps you are an experienced sales professional looking to sharpen your skills, maybe you run a business and are looking to get your way more often or perhaps you liked the beautifully designed cover and felt obliged to take a look inside. One thing I am certain of, though, is that your getting even this far in the book tells me that you are open-minded about change and are serious about your personal success.

Throughout my studies of people, human relationships and business interactions, I have been amazed by how some people achieve dramatically different results than others with what seem to be the exact same ingredients.

In businesses in which people have identical products and resources, some people struggle to find customers, and yet others cannot stop finding more success. Despite their differences in attitude and endeavor, these successful people, I have learned, have one thing in common: they know exactly what to say, how to say it and how to make it count.

This realization has had me fascinated with the difference a subtle change of words can make to the outcome of a whole conversation, and it has fueled my study of the precise triggers that cause a shift in a person's belief system.

Back in 2012, I published a tiny book called *Magic Words*, following the words I feature heavily in my training and speeches. It is a book I am really proud of, and not just because this little book made many bestseller lists. More importantly, the people who bought it actually went on to read it, use what they learned and get great results from employing simple changes in their word choices.

Let me explain a little about what these Magic Words are.

Magic Words are sets of words that talk straight to the subconscious brain. The subconscious brain is a powerful tool in decision-making because it is preprogrammed through our conditioning to make decisions without overanalyzing them. It works a little like a computer—it has only "yes" and "no" outputs and can never land on a "maybe." It is strong and decisive and moves quickly. Using words that talk straight to the part of the brain that is free from maybes and responds on reflex gives you a fair advantage in conversation and can result in you getting your own way more often.

EXAMPLES

If you are looking for examples of where your subconscious has served you, here are some simple ones:

Controlling your breathing while you sleep.

....

Assisting your routine on a familiar journey.

....

Allowing your attention to be immediately drawn to anything that resembles your name.

....

We all rely on our subconscious brain daily to get us through everything that happens without us having to process, compute and take care of every decision all by ourselves.

In this book, I revisit some of those Magic Words, add some new ones and provide you with precise examples to show you how to apply them to your conversations. I do all I can to help you understand the principles behind the chosen words and allow you to find greater application for them in your life.

These words are tried, tested and proven to deliver results when applied properly. This book is about far more than just Magic Words, however. As you work through each section, you will receive powerful insight into what makes people tick and learn how simple changes you can apply instantly can make your life so much easier. Yes, the advice is aimed at increasing your business success, but every principle discussed is easily transferable into any industry and every area of life, to help you become more persuasive and influential and have a bigger impact in all that you do.

My advice is to have a notebook and pen with you when you read. Look to create your own examples as you work through each section. Then make the decision to try them for yourself as soon as possible, getting more comfortable and confident each time you do. Everything I share may sound simple, but simple does not necessarily mean easy. Get comfortable being uncomfortable. I am excited to hear about your results, so please connect with me on your chosen social platform and share your experiences of becoming a more skilled decision catalyst, ensuring more of your conversations really count.

1

I'm Not Sure If It's for You, But

One of the most common reasons I hear from people as to why they fail to introduce their idea, product or service to others is the fact that they are fearful of the rejection they might receive.

It was for this reason that I figured the best place to start is with a set of Magic Words you can use to introduce something to just about anybody, at just about any point in time, that is completely rejection-free. The words in question are, "I'm not sure if it's for you, but . . ."

Let's take a moment to understand how this simple structure works.

Opening a statement with the words, "I'm not sure if it's for you," causes the listener's subconscious brain to hear, "There's no pressure here." By suggesting that they may not be interested, you naturally increase their intrigue. They wonder what "it" is, and this spike in curiosity hooks them. What's more, it fires an internal driver that tells them a decision needs to be made, and the soft approach ensures this decision feels unpressured and internal.

The real magic, though, is delivered through the final three-letter word of this sequence, a word that typically should be avoided in all conversations: the word "but."

Imagine receiving a comment from your employer that started with the words, "You know that you're a really valuable member of the team. We love everything that you do here, but some things need to change." What's the only part you would remember? I am guessing the part that you would focus on most is everything that follows "but." The word "but" negates everything that was said prior, so when you say to somebody, "I'm not sure if it's for you, but...," what the little voice inside your listener's head hears is, "You might want to look at this."

When you say to somebody, "I'm not sure if it's for you, but...," the little voice inside your listener's head hears, "You might want to look at this."

EXAMPLES

Here are a few examples to help you in your daily routine:

I'm not sure if it's for you, but would you happen to know someone who is interested in (insert the results of your product or service)?

....

I'm not sure if it's for you, but we have plans on Saturday, and you're welcome to join us.

....

I'm not sure if it's for you, but this option is available for this month only, and I would hate for you to miss out.

....

This rejection-free approach creates a simple outcome. One of two things happens: your listener leans in and asks for more information because they are personally interested, or, in the very, very worst-case scenario, they say they will give it some thought.

2

Open-Minded

If you were to ask a room of a thousand people whether they considered themselves open-minded, I am sure over nine hundred of them would raise their hands.

Just about everybody in the land thinks of themselves as meeting this criterion, and it's pretty easy to understand why.

When the alternative is being considered "closed-minded," this perception of choice is almost guaranteed to steer others toward your idea. Knowing that people like to see themselves as open-minded, you can easily give yourself a fair advantage within your conversations. When introducing a brand-new idea to a stranger, friend, prospect or team member, using the words, "How open-minded are you?" and following up that sentence with a scenario you want them to opt into allows you to naturally attract people toward the very thing that you are looking for their support with. This preface shifts you from having fifty-fifty odds of them agreeing with you to odds of ninety-ten in your favor. Everybody wants to be open-minded.

EXAMPLES

Here are a few examples of the words in practice:

How open-minded would you be about trying this as an alternative?

_____

Would you be open-minded about giving this a chance?

_____

How open-minded are you about increasing your monthly income?

_____

Would you be open-minded about seeing if we could work together?

_____

Each of these options makes it very difficult for the other person to reject your idea, and it at least makes them feel obligated to explore the possibility. It seems like you are giving them a choice, when really you are heavily weighting the only option you are giving them. Put simply, "How open-minded are you about at least trying it?"

When introducing a new idea, start with, "How open-minded are you?" This will naturally attract people toward the very thing that you'd like them to support. Everybody wants to be open-minded.

3
What Do You Know?

How often do you find yourself in a conversation that quickly becomes a debate because you are speaking with someone who thinks they know best and perhaps even wishes to lecture you with their opinions?

To influence others, you must be aware of how to control a conversation. One way of regaining control is to move the other person's position from one of certainty to one of doubt.

Typically people try to create this position of uncertainty through directly challenging the other person's opinion and perhaps even entering into an argument. I am sure you have had moments when you have been frustrated by someone's inability to understand what you are saying and flustered that you cannot overcome their preconceptions. This can happen regularly when you are trying to introduce new ideas or concepts, and the "I know best" mentality of many people can be difficult to overcome.

The best way to overcome the "I know best" mentality of many people is to **question the knowledge on which the other person's opinion was founded.**

I am certain that you want to stop people from arguing with you, so this situation could regularly result in you backing down or walking away. For an opinion to have merit, however, it really should be founded on some form of knowledge. The best way to overcome this kind of conflict is not to win the argument; instead, you must question the knowledge on which the other person's opinion was founded. The goal is to turn the situation into one in which the other person admits that their opinion was based on insufficient evidence, while retaining the ability for them to save face in the conversation. It is the power in the preface, "What do you know about...?" that softly threatens their knowledge base and forces them to share the reference on which their argument is based. Often this results in them realizing their strong opinion was unfounded.

EXAMPLES

Examples you could use in the real world are…

What do you know about us, our business and the way we do things differently?

....

What do you know about everything that has changed since (insert event)?

....

What do you know about how things really work here?

....

What do you know about the benefits of (insert product sector)?

....

These questions allow the other person to realize their opinion is perhaps not correct, and they can quickly become far more receptive to change.

The worst that can happen is that you learn the precise basis of their argument and can then position your point in contrast to it. Use words like this to challenge others with confidence and avoid arguments that always end with losers since, regardless of who the loser is, you are unlikely to leave with your desired result. Either everybody wins, or everybody loses.

4

How Would You Feel If?

A word that gets thrown around like confetti in conferences is "motivation," yet still, when I ask my audiences to share with me what the word means, all I see in response are blank faces.

It is the meaning of this word that creates the true base for understanding all areas of negotiation, influence and persuasion, and you should explore it further if you would like to perform at your peak.

Put simply, understanding this word would mean that you could probably get just about anybody to do just about anything.

The word motivation derives from two very common words forced together. The first part of the word, the "motiv-" part, is derived from the Latin word "motivus," the modern-day translation of which is "motive." Another word for motive is "reason." The "-ation" part of the word derives from "action," and if somebody is going to take action, they are going to do something or move. This means that a very simple definition of motivation is "a reason to move" or "a reason to do."

Now ask yourself this: would it be fair to say that if the reason were big enough, you could get just about anybody to do just about anything?

If you want people to do things that typically they do not want to do, first you need to find an honest reason that is big enough. Understanding what reasons are big enough means you have to understand how people are motivated. People are motivated by one of two things: either avoiding a loss or acquiring a potential gain. They either want to go toward the light, the good thing that they are looking for, or they want to get away from the thing that could potentially hurt them. The real world tells us that people will work far harder to avoid a potential loss than they will to achieve a potential gain. Greater than that is the fact that the more contrast you can create between where somebody does not want to be and where they hope to be, the more likely you are to get people to move. Understanding the truth of motivation, coupled with this next point, gives you real context for this set of Magic Words.

The second thing you must consider is whether people base their decisions on emotion or logic. The true answer to that question is, in fact, both; it is just that the decision is always made for emotive reasons first.

The real world tells us that people will work far harder to avoid a potential loss than they will to achieve a potential gain.

Something has to feel right before it ever makes sense. I am sure you have stepped away from a conversation confused about why the other person did not follow your advice and have wondered, "I don't know why they don't do it. It just makes sense for them to do it." If you are trying to win the argument based on your advice making sense, you are calling out to the wrong set of reasons. People make decisions based on what feels right first. If you can make it feel right, the rest is easy.

Understanding those two complex theories is the foundation for this set of Magic Words, and it is all brought together in a preface to a question. By introducing a future scenario with the words, "How would you feel if…?" you allow the other person to time travel to that moment and imagine the emotions that would be triggered at that point. Choosing moments that trigger both positive and negative emotions will allow you to create a truth worth changing for. It will also prepare others to accept your ideas on how to help them achieve success or avoid loss. What you then create is a conditional future-facing scenario, something they can see for themselves.

Examples might be something like…

How would you feel if this decision led to your promotion?

....

How would you feel if your competition passed you?

....

How would you feel if you turned this around?

....

How would you feel if you lost everything?

....

What about this one: how would you feel if this time next year you were debt-free, living in your dream home and planning your next vacation?

Creating these conditional future scenarios using the words, "How would you feel if…?" gets people excited about their future and gives them a reason to move either toward the good news or away from the bad news. Remember, the greater the contrast, the more likely you are to get that someone to move.

5
Just Imagine

Did you know that every decision any human makes is made at least twice? The decision is first made in your mind hypothetically before it is ever made in reality.

In fact, for a decision to come true, you must have first at least imagined yourself doing it. Have you ever been in a situation in which you have said, or even just mouthed, these words back to somebody else: "I just couldn't see myself doing that"?

It is a literal thing. If you cannot see yourself doing something, the chances of you doing it are slim to none. People make decisions based on the images they see in their minds, so if you can place pictures in people's minds, then you can use the results of those images to influence their decisions.

Creating pictures in the minds of others is done by telling stories. We remember as children many a good story that started with the words, "Once upon a time…" When we heard those words, we knew it was time to kick back, enjoy the moment and embrace our imagination while someone used words to paint a world for us to jump into. It would be really tough to engage adults with that same powerful preface, so you need some Magic Words that create the same picturesque outcome. When you hear the words, "Just imagine," the subconscious brain kicks a switch and opens up the image viewer, and it cannot help but picture the very scenario you are creating.

In the previous section you learned about away motivation and toward motivation. You can apply those same exact rules to how you finish off your "just imagine" scenarios to help drive people to do the things you would like them to do.

Here are some examples: **EXAMPLES**

Just imagine how things will be in six months' time once you have implemented this.

Just imagine what your boss would say if you missed this opportunity.

Just imagine the look on your kids' faces when they see you achieve this.

Just imagine the impact this could have.

Allowing the power attached to the other person's creative mind to build your case for you will always save you guessing and can create a more vivid reality than anything you could possibly describe. Let them do the hard work. Imagine saying to a team member or prospect, "Just imagine the smiles on your kids' faces when you tell them you've booked a trip to Disneyland," or, "Just imagine stepping up on stage and picking up that big incentive check," or, "Just imagine pulling into the driveway in your brand-new car." As you make those statements, they will see the picture of that very thing happening. Now that they have seen the thing, chances are their belief in achieving it goes through the roof. I mean, just imagine the difference that is going to have for you and your business.

Creating pictures in the minds of others is done by telling stories. When you hear "Just imagine," the brain pictures the very scenario you are creating.

6
When Would
Be a Good Time?

This simple set of words
helps us overcome one of the
biggest challenges you face
when trying to get people
to take a serious look at your
product, service or idea.

One of the biggest reasons your ideas fail to get heard is that others tell you that they just don't have the time to consider them.

By using the preface, "When would be a good time to…?" you prompt the other person to subconsciously assume that there will be a good time and that no is not an option. This assumption acknowledges that there will be a time when this can definitely fit into their schedule and that it is just a case of confirming the specific time and date. It is this kind of direct question that prevents people from telling you that they have not got the time and, as a result, helps you avoid one of the biggest objections people face.

EXAMPLES

Examples for you to use include...

When would be a good time for you to take a proper look at this?

When would be a good time to get started?

When would be a good time to speak next?

In all of these scenarios, please be certain that when you gain a reply, you work to schedule the precise next point of contact in order to keep control of the conversation in your hands.

When you do get around to following up or speaking again at the agreed time, please do not ask them what they thought about what you asked them to look at. This makes it easy for them to talk bad news or bring up their concerns. Instead, swap that question with, "So, what do you like about it?" and watch them list the good-news reasons instead.

The preface "When would be a good time to ...?" prompts the other person **to assume that there will be a good time and that no is not an option.**

7

I'm Guessing You Haven't Got Around To

Sticking to the theme of following up with people, I thought I'd share some words that you can use in those scenarios in which you are fearful of contacting the other person because you think they have not done the thing you would like them to do.

You know the times when you have sent over some details or they have said they needed to consult with someone else, and now you need to make contact to take the next step?

When you are fearful that somebody has not done something, instead of asking them how that thing went, you may want to start the conversation slightly differently.

Open the conversation by allowing the other person to save face, but also by preventing them from using any of the excuses you think they might use. This leaves them with nowhere to go in the conversation other than where you would like them to go. The reason they cannot use the excuses is because you have been bold enough to start the conversation in a way that suggests they were about to use the very excuse they had prepared: by prefacing your question with, "I'm guessing you haven't got around to…"

Imagine you are making a telephone call to someone who said they needed to consult with their partner before making a decision.

If you ask, "I'm guessing you haven't got around to speaking to your partner yet?" it now becomes impossible for them to use that excuse. They respond in one of two ways: either they feel proud that they have done what they had promised, or they are embarrassed that they haven't and make a new promise to put right that fact.

Other examples could be... **EXAMPLES**

I'm guessing you haven't got around to looking over the documents yet?

I'm guessing you haven't got around to setting a date yet?

I'm guessing you haven't got around to making a decision yet?

By pushing for the negative scenario, you get people to rise to the positive or to tell you how they are going to fix the thing they said they were going to do.

By using the words you are fearful they may give you back in the other direction, you create a scenario that completely disarms them. If you say to somebody, "I'm guessing you haven't got around to making a decision on this yet," and they say, "No, you're right. We're still thinking about it," you can open up the negotiation. If, instead, they say, "No, we have, and we've made a decision," you can say, "Great, when are we ready to get started?"

By pushing for the negative scenario, you get them to rise to the positive or to tell you how they are going to fix the thing they said they were going to do, because most people are people of their word and feel pretty bad when they are called out for it.

8
Simple Swaps

Using a simple technique, I am going to provide two pieces of magic in one short section. The psychology behind this technique, which involves turning an open question into a closed one, results in you receiving a guaranteed outcome or answer.

It came to me, first of all, from trying to prevent a giant mistake I see so many people make when they reach the end of a sales presentation.

Following many a presentation, the question people reach for is, "Do you have any questions?" Asking this creates the subconscious suggestion that the other person *should* have questions, and if they don't, it makes them feel peculiar and perhaps even a little stupid. This encourages them to leave the decision-making conversation and go away to think about it.

A simple change of wording puts you in control. Swap the phrase, "Do you have any questions?" with the improved, "What questions do you have for me?"

A simple change of wording moves this from out of your control to completely in your control. Swap the phrase, "Do you have any questions?" with the improved, "What questions do you have for me?" The minute you assume an outcome, the easiest response for them to give is that they have no questions. What does this really mean? It means they have made a decision and you are perfectly positioned to ask for it. This change of wording typically results in you gaining that response or in the specific questions they need answers to.

Either way, you are far closer to a decision, and you avoid the dreaded, "I need some time to think about it."

That was the first simple lesson, but I promised two for one in this section. This next change is so simple and so profound, it works whether spoken, written, by text message... it works everywhere. It's best used when you are looking to garner an additional piece of information from the other person and you want it effortlessly. Consider a scenario in which you have met someone and would like to have a conversation with them at a later time. A mistake many people make is asking, "Can I have your phone number?" When you ask somebody, "Can I have your...?" it creates a permission-based resistance in the other person, which makes it harder to get what you hoped for, since a "yes" or "no" response is required. It can be seen as an invasion of privacy. Instead, asking the alternative question, "What's the best number to contact you at?" results in people effortlessly giving you the information you requested.

Both of these sets of Magic Words demonstrate how changing a couple of words can make all the difference in the results you get from your conversations.

Changing a couple of words can make all the difference in the results you get from your conversations.

9
You Have Three Options

People hate to feel manipulated and nearly always want to feel like they made the final decision. When someone needs help deciding, using these words can help narrow their gaze, reduce their choices and make it easier for them to pick.

The words, "As I see it, you have three options," help the other person through the decision-making process and allow you to appear impartial in doing so.

You are simply presenting them with their options, yet you now have the opportunity to display them in a way that favors your preferred choice. The rhythm of three makes for easy listening for the other person, and by leaving your preferred choice until the end, you easily build the value of that option and load the choices so your preferred outcome stands out as a clear favorite.

For sure, we could play with several examples. In fact, we could probably think of dozens that relate to your life, but here's one to help your thinking.

EXAMPLE

Imagine you are looking for someone to join your business or organization and they are on the fence about it. Start by making a statement that sets the scene for the real-life scenario. That statement might run something like this:

"So, you are currently in a job that you kind of hate. You're not enjoying it so much, the hours are long, it's keeping you away from your family and the money is nowhere near what you would like it to be. We have shown you a business opportunity and you like it, yet you are not sure exactly what to do.

"As I see it, you have three options. First, you could look for another job, work on your résumé, send out applications, go through interviews and work through that entire process to perhaps find another employer offering a similar package and more than likely expecting the same kind of work for the same return. Second, you could do absolutely nothing, stay exactly where you are right now, accept that your current circumstances are as good as it gets and just suck it up. Or third, you could give this a try, work it alongside what you're doing right now and see how far you go.

"Of those three options, what's going to be easier for you?" Finishing with another set of Magic Words means they have to pick one of those options.

"What's going to be easier for you?" means that the laborious new-job option is off the table. Since staying put was already off the table, the only option they have left is the easy one—the one you want them to pick; the one you left to the end and stacked in your favor because you made that the path of least resistance. So, start with, "You have three options," finish with, "What's going to be easier for you?" and watch people effortlessly pick the choice that previously they were finding so difficult to make.

10
Two Types of People

As entrepreneurs, sales professionals and business owners, we are often tasked with the responsibility of helping people to make their minds up.

To me, the primary job description of all sales professionals is to be "decision catalysts" in the lives of their customers and prospects, yet still the job can be more simply described as "professional mind-maker-upper."

There are many people who do a great job of getting people interested in something, yet it is the final moment of helping people to decide that creates the action that drives results. That is the tough part.

Help people to choose by removing some of the choices and creating easy options. Decisions become easier when the choices are polarizing. Red or white wine, beach or ski vacation, rom-com or action— all become simpler decisions than the broader alternative. Your goal is to create a statement that presents choice and then to allow the other person to pick.

Asking people to decide for themselves who they are with the Magic Words "two types of people" prompts a near-instant decision. The second someone hears, "There are two types of people in this world," the little voice in their head immediately wonders which one they are, and they wait with bated breath to hear the choices.

EXAMPLES

Now your role is to deliver them two choices and make one of them stand out as the easy option. Here are just a few examples:

There are two types of people in this world: those who leave their personal financial success in the hands of their employers and those who take full responsibility and build their own futures.

There are two types of people in this world: those who judge something before they have even tried it and those who are prepared to try something and base their opinion on their own experience.

There are two types of people in this world: those who resist change in favor of nostalgia and those who move with the times and create a better future.

You should be able to see the pattern in the examples and understand how the options are clearly stacked in favor of the decision you would like them to pick.

Something for you to think about as a reader is that there are two types of people in this world: those who read books like this and do nothing and those who put what they read into practice and enjoy immediate results.

11

I Bet You're a
Bit Like Me

This set of words is possibly
one of my favorites because it
can help just about anybody
agree to just about anything.
It is even more powerful in a
conversation with a stranger
than it is with somebody you
already know.

When you are talking to a stranger, the conversation needs to move easily, which means it typically follows the path of least resistance.

If you use this preface ahead of a scenario you would like people to believe to be true, expect them to agree with you wholeheartedly, quickly and easily. Prefacing a statement with the Magic Words, "I bet you're a bit like me," quite often results in the other person comfortably agreeing with what you are saying, providing that you are reasonable.

This serves as a wonderful tool to help gather evidence to use in building your later recommendations. My experience has taught me that many customers, prospects and people in general are not always completely honest. Getting them to provide evidence that supports your objective makes it harder for them to disagree with you. You can use this set of words to help avoid many common objections by gaining full agreement with something they may otherwise have tried to use as a future excuse.

EXAMPLES

Imagine you are fearful of someone objecting to your idea because they don't have the time to commit to it. Early in the conversation you could say something like...

I bet you're a bit like me: you enjoy working hard now, knowing that it will pay dividends in the future.

I bet you're a bit like me: you hate watching trashy TV in the evening and would rather work on something beneficial.

I bet you're a bit like me: you're a busy person who's always juggling to get everything done.

Slip those kinds of statements into early conversations while holding eye contact with the other person, and just watch them nod back at you. When they do, this means they know that you know they agree with those concepts. This makes it an awful lot harder for them to tell you they have not got the time to do what you demonstrated could give them the things they said they want.

The Magic Words "I bet you're a bit like me" often result in **the other person comfortably agreeing with you.**

12
If... Then

Our speech patterns, listening patterns and, in turn, belief systems are all preprogrammed and hardwired into us throughout our childhood—

so much so that the repetitive patterns of words we receive through to our adolescence create habits, systems inside of our belief systems, that we lean on in order to support our personal decision-making process.

An example of this is a simple pattern of speech that appeared a lot in your youth, and its impact is often overlooked. Adults made many conditional statements to us when we were children, such as . . .

If you don't eat all your dinner, then you're not going to get any dessert.

If you don't study hard at school, then you're not going to get into the college or job you're hoping for.

If you don't tidy your room, then you're going to be grounded for the weekend.

EXAMPLES

When they made conditional statements like these to you, chances are that you believed them. These statements hold power over our beliefs and actions.

As a consequence, creating a scenario using the preface "if" and adding a second scenario with the preface "then" means that people are highly likely to believe the outcome.

If you decide to give this a try, then I promise you won't be disappointed.

If you put this in your stores, then I am certain your customers will like it.

If you give me a chance in the role, then I am confident you will thank me later.

By creating these "if … then" sandwiches, you can position guaranteed outcomes that are very difficult not to believe. If you are prepared to give this a try, then I am certain you will see the results as early as the first day you try it.

13

Don't Worry

What I love best about this
next set of simple words
is the power they have on
people who are nervous,
apprehensive or showing
signs of concern.

You know when you can see and feel the anxiety in somebody, when they are uncertain about what to do next or perhaps even fearful. These two Magic Words provide instant relief, and you can typically see the change in the recipient.

Say the words, "Don't worry," and the tension just pours out of them as they become more relaxed. Just two words that, when said confidently and calmly, create an outcome that is the equivalent of the expression "Phew!"—that little sigh that comes out as they start to feel in control.

This is particularly useful in high-stress scenarios, when confronted with someone who is panicked or just to comfortably put someone at ease. The minute somebody is indecisive, hold your posture, stay relaxed and give them the feeling that you have this under control and can help them navigate the next step.

EXAMPLES

Examples include…

Don't worry. You're bound to be nervous right now.

Don't worry, I know you don't know what to do right now, but that's what I'm here for. I'm here to help you through this process and overcome all the hurdles as they crop up along the way.

Don't worry. I felt just the way you feel right now before I started, and look at me now.

So, don't worry if you're wondering how you're going to make all these new word choices stick. They will come in time, and you will have soon mastered it after getting a little better from one conversation to the next.

"Don't worry" is particularly useful in high-stress scenarios, when confronted with someone who is panicked—it puts people at ease.

14

Most People

These two words, which contain just ten letters, are possibly responsible for more of my negotiating success than any other single strategy I have employed in my businesses.

Indecision is the biggest thing that stands in the way of progress, and these words can help jump people out of procrastination in a flash.

There are a few things that are worth understanding about people, and these are two big ones.

First, people take great confidence from the fact that people like them have made a decision before them and that that decision worked out just fine.

Consider this scenario, maybe one you have experienced yourself. On vacation, you see a group of children on top of a rock face looking to jump into the water below, but nobody wants to go first. However, as soon as one person is brave enough to go first and jumps into the water, lands with a splash and doesn't suffer any injury but instead breaks the surface with a great big smile on their face, now everybody seems to think it is a good idea. Human beings, people, you and I—we all like to follow others and trust that there is safety in numbers.

Second, sometimes people need to be told what to do, but without their permission it can sound rude. I am sure there have been plenty of times that you have wanted to say, "What I think you should do is…"

These two factors create the power in the application of the Magic Words "most people." Now when you are faced with a moment when what you want to say is, "Look, what I think you should do is this," but you cannot say that because it is kind of obnoxious, instead you can simply state what "most people" would do in this situation and watch how it changes everything.

When you tell people what most people would do, their subconscious brain says, "Aha, I'm most people, so if that is what most people would do, then perhaps that is what I should do too."

When you tell people what most people would do, their brain says, **"I'm most people, so perhaps that is what I should do too."**

EXAMPLES

The examples for this are endless:

What most people do is complete the forms with me here today. You then receive your welcome pack and we get you booked in for a launch.

What most people do is place a small order to get started, commit to a few of the best products, see how they work out in their daily routines and then decide what they want to do next.

Most people in your circumstances would grab this opportunity with both hands, knowing that there is almost no risk.

Try to argue with each of these points and see how much they can be used to strengthen your point of view. In fact, most people put the words "most people" into some of their daily conversations, and most of those people see an immediate positive effect on their influence.

Most people put the words "most people" into their daily conversations, **and most of those people see an immediate positive effect.**

15
The Good News

Now is the time for us to talk about how you can turn around all that negative energy—the negative energy that comes from others in your team, others who you are prospecting or perhaps just other people in your life.

These words provide you with a tool to spin a negative into a positive using a technique called labeling.

The moment you apply a label to something, it becomes almost impossible for the other person in the conversation to shed that label.

It is the acceptance of this new label that creates the ability to change the direction of a conversation with minimal effort and move it toward a more positive outcome.

Using the Magic Words, "The good news is…" as a preface to your chosen point ensures that the recipient has to accept the label you have attached to it. This optimistic spin can help you face negativity in your life, prevents you from ending up in a self-sabotaging conversation of blame and pity and helps you start to build in a new direction.

If somebody is questioning their ability to do something, then you can respond with, "Look, the good news is that we have dozens of people who were in exactly the same situation when they first started, and they have gone on to be successful and are here to support you, too."

If they are unsure whether they have got the skills that are required in order to make the business work, you could say, "The good news is that we have comprehensive training you can complete at your own pace to give you all the skills you need to make a success of this business."

What about when somebody is resisting change but says they want more success? You could respond with, "The good news is you already know that what you are doing now is not working, so what is the harm in trying this?"

By prefacing things with, "The good news is...," you cause people to face forward with optimism and zap any negative energy out of the conversation.

By prefacing things with, "The good news is...," you cause people to face forward with optimism and zap any negative energy out of the conversation.

By bringing more positivity to situations with, "The good news is . . ." and responding with, "That's great," you soon start shifting the balance in people's thoughts.

You can use this same principle with two more words when faced with people who give excuses or reasons as to why they are not ready to move forward.

When somebody gives you an excuse, they expect you to push back and argue around that point. Next time somebody tells you a reason why they do not want to do something, respond by saying, "That's great." When somebody says, "I couldn't do it because of this," say, "That's great, you've just found out another way that doesn't work," and watch how they look at you differently. You have changed the way that they think. Now, some of them might think that you have completely lost it, but hey, you probably did not want those people in your life anyway.

By bringing more positivity to situations with, "The good news is..." and responding with, "That's great," you soon start shifting the balance in people's thoughts and allow them to question themselves toward a better outcome and behavior.

16
What Happens Next

Let's apply some context that happens in many business-related discussions.

You have created an opportunity, got a red-hot prospect, been out, shown them how you can help them and walked them through your entire presentation, and now you are at the point where they have nodded and smiled all the way through everything you've presented to them.

You want them to commit, but following all of this relationship building and imparting of knowledge, the conversation grinds to a stop with nobody leading the actual decision.

This happens far too often, and it is a product of people being so fearful of being seen as pushy or controlling that they fail to finish the job they started. It can be all too easy to leave the decision-making up to other people and hope that they will make the right choice, but without your help, often others make no decision at all and everyone loses out.

In these consultative discussions, it is your responsibility to lead the conversation, and following the sharing of the required information, your role is to move it toward a close.

You need to let them know what happens next, so the Magic Words you require are precisely that: "What happens next is…" This is a perfect way of linking all of the information they need to make a decision, the information you provided when you presented to them, and bringing them through to the completion that needs to follow. So, what you do is create a scene. You do not ask them what they would like to do; you just tell them what happens next.

"What happens next is that we are going to take a few moments, complete some of your personal details and get things set up for you to receive everything in the quickest possible time.

"Then we need to schedule another meeting for us to get started, and at that point I am going to help you through all the steps to ensure that you realize your goals and are fully aware of all the support that is available to you. In terms of registering your details, what is the best address for you?"

It is your responsibility to lead the conversation, and following the sharing of the required information, your role is to move it toward a close.

The easier the question is to answer, the easier you gain your decision.

Finishing this process with a question that is effortless to answer is the key to gaining a rapid response and a positive outcome.

In the example just discussed, you should see how, just by asking them that simple question at the end, the second they respond with their address, it means they are moving forward with your proposal.

You could comfortably ask any type of question to close your scenario. The easier the question is to answer, the easier you gain your decision. Having a concise and constructive "what happens next" conversation will mean that you successfully close far more conversations in the first meeting and make more happen in the moments that you have with people.

17

What Makes You Say That?

Objections are a common part of everyday life. We face indecision from others in our personal and professional lives and quite often find ourselves having to accept another person's idea.

These conversations can become confrontational, so to avoid argument, the majority of people are happy to let go of their goal in favor of an easy life.

To overcome an objection, you must first understand what an objection really is. There is always the possibility that an objection is an alternative to saying, "No thank you," or a way of pushing the decision away for another day. However, it is always a shift in control of the conversation, and the second any objection is raised, the other person seizes power and you are obliged to respond to their wishes.

Success in negotiating is all about maintaining control in a conversation, and the person in control is always the person who is asking the questions. By treating every objection you face as nothing more than a question, you can quickly regain control of the conversation by asking a question in return.

EXAMPLES

In a business setting, common objections include...

I haven't got the time.

....

It's the wrong time.

....

I want to shop around.

....

I haven't got the money right now.

....

I need to speak to somebody else before I make a decision about this.

....

The worst thing that you could do when such an objection is raised is to respond with your counterargument and make statements that disprove their current opinion. Instead, you can tackle each of these common objections effectively by being inquisitive about them and asking a question in the opposite direction.

Success in negotiating is all about maintaining control in a conversation, and **the person in control is always the person who is asking the questions.**

Of course, you could develop unique and precise questions to challenge every objection you are faced with. Alternatively, you can lean on the one set of Magic Words that has served in millions of similar scenarios: "What makes you say that?"

EXAMPLES

Here are a few examples:

The customer says, "I need to speak to somebody else before I make a decision about this." You say, "What makes you say that?"

The customer says, "Really, I don't have all the money right now." You say, "What makes you say that?"

The customer says, "I'm really not sure I've got the time to fit this in around what I'm doing right now." You say, "What makes you say that?"

This shift of control now leaves the other person obligated to give an answer and fill in the gaps in their previous statement.

It prevents you from making prejudgments or entering into an argument, and it allows you to better understand their point of view before recommending a next thought or action.

What you are asking them to do is to explain themselves properly. The words, "What makes you say that?" mean they now have to take responsibility and explain what they really mean. Having this explained properly puts you in a position in which you can then help them with their decision or at least have a greater understanding of why they cannot make it at this time.

18
Before You Make Your Mind Up

Moving somebody from a "no" to a "yes" is nearly impossible. Before you can move someone to full agreement, your first action is to move them to a position of "maybe."

When you find yourself in a position in which the other person is leaning toward not choosing your idea, you can quickly move them back in your direction by prefacing your next action with another set of Magic Words: "Before you make your mind up…"

EXAMPLES

Here are some examples of how you can use these words to keep the conversation alive:

Look, **before** you make your mind up, let's make sure we've looked at all the facts.

Before you make your mind up, why don't we just run through the details one more time so you can know what it is that you are saying no to?

Before you make your mind up, wouldn't it make sense to speak to a few more people about the difference this could make for you and your family?

These simple examples can often move people from a position of no and allow the negotiation to continue by making them look at it from a different perspective. It is this shift in vantage point that then allows you to add alternative information to support your idea and increase your influence over their decision.

19

If I Can, Will You?

Have you ever been in one of those scenarios in which your prospect or customer pushes back with reasons as to why they cannot do the thing you would like them to do?

Perhaps they are looking for you to make a change from your standard terms or they would like you to offer an improved price.

This same thing appears in our personal lives when people make excuses about why they cannot make it to events or celebrations.

These situations are created by the other person delivering an external condition that is affecting their ability to move forward with your idea. They have removed themselves from the process and abdicated responsibility to something out of their control.

You have the power in these situations to isolate this condition and remove the barrier by responding with a powerful question that eliminates their argument. This is achieved by using the question structure, "If I can…, then will you…?"

Imagine that you want a friend to join you for a night out next Friday. Your friend says the reason they cannot join you is because the car is in for repair and the buses do not run that late. You could eliminate this challenge with the question,

"If I can pick you up and drop you off at home, then will you be able to be ready for seven pm?"

The same principle can be used when someone is looking for you to reduce your price in line with a competitive offer.

"If I can match that price for you, then would you be happy to place the order with me today?"

In both of these scenarios, you are still not obligated to meet the condition presented, but you are in control of what happens next. You may receive further reasons and honesty from the other person that prevents you moving forward, or you may find that you gain their agreement. With their agreement to the condition, you can now present your best option to them and will be far more likely to reach your desired outcome.

You have the power in these situations to remove the barrier by responding with a powerful question that eliminates the other person's argument.

20
Enough

This next word relates precisely to scenarios in which you are looking for others to make decisions on quantity or level of service.

It's all about making it a lot easier for the other person to reach a little higher than they may have done otherwise.

Taking the example of retail sales, there are countless occasions in which customers deliberate over the quantity they should purchase of certain items. You can probably even relate: for instance, maybe at the grocery store you have questioned the number of apples you should buy.

In every set of circumstances in which you involve yourself in the decision-making process, you have the power to influence the actions of others. Consumers love to be led through the right thing to do, and assisting people in making their minds up is a skill that will help you reach the highest places.

Jumping back to the scenario in the grocery store, let's imagine that you are deliberating between four and eight apples. If you were being served in that transaction and were asked the direct question, "Would eight apples be enough for you?" your instant response would be "yes," and the decision would be made.

In business, your goal can be to have people come back for your products time and time again. Ensuring that they have the correct quantities to make a habit of using your products can be a key component of that. I am sure that you have enjoyed the use of travel-sized toiletries but never gone on to invest in the products yourself, yet when you have purchased a three-for-two offer, this has often become your new brand of choice.

There is a company that I have worked extensively with, and their key product is a drinking gel that they want people to come back and consume time and time again. In face-to-face discussions with a customer, the dilemma often arises over how many bottles they should purchase, and the choice typically sits between two and three bottles. Instead of a detailed analysis of the benefits of three bottles over two, you can easily simplify the decision with the direct question, "Would three bottles be enough for you?"

In every set of circum-stances in which you involve yourself in the decision-making process, you have the power to influence the actions of others.

Integrating this principle into all conversations involving your business can have a huge impact on your results. **Just imagine if every transaction contained one more unit.**

This use of words drives the recipient to answer the direct question, and "yes" becomes the path of least resistance.

When used skillfully in situations in which somebody impressionable must choose between two options, you will almost always get them to pick the bigger one.

I am sure you can think of many similar scenarios in your own business. Understand that if you offer someone the choice between two numbers, you are likely to receive a fifty-fifty response. Yet a direct question involving only the larger option and the Magic Word "enough" swings those odds far further in your direction. Integrating this principle into all conversations involving your business can have a huge impact on your results. Just imagine if every transaction contained just one more unit.

21
Just One More Thing

In sales training programs, it is typical to talk about the importance of an "upsell": inviting your consumer to purchase more at the point of transaction.

The previous section showed a simple way of achieving this, yet a practice that is less common is the downsell. A downsell involves working on achieving a lesser objective if you fail to meet your primary objective in a conversation.

Perhaps you went in looking for agreement to a large long-term contract; a downsell may be a first trial order. Or perhaps you wanted someone to partner with your business; the downsell could be to try your products as a customer.

This set of Magic Words allows you to create that opportunity on your way out of a conversation. Instead of leaving with nothing, you use these words for a further attempt. This technique was first introduced to me when watching crime dramas on TV at my grandparents' house as a child. These shows introduced me to possibly the greatest negotiator I have ever met, the television detective Columbo, who was famous for a precise set of words.

What he would do is quiz his suspect, go through the rigmarole of gathering all the information he could and then turn to leave.

Just when the suspect was sure they had got away with things, Columbo would turn back to them and, with his finger pointed upward, say, "Oh, just one more thing." It was in this moment, when the suspect's guard was now down, that he could ask his next question and receive the key information that he needed—the clue that would lead him to solve the crime.

Using the Magic Words "Just one more thing" keeps the conversation alive and can help you avoid leaving with nothing.

This lesson can translate into many scenarios in our lives. Here is just one of them.

You meet with someone to introduce them to your ideas and look to gain their commitment. They kind of like you and your ideas, but they are not so sure, and the meeting is coming to a close. You thank them for their time, pack your things up and head for the door. At this point you could create a Columbo moment and turn back to them with the words, "Just one more thing." When they think that they have got away with not buying anything, you introduce a simple idea, something that is really easy for them to try, and bring them into your world with a far smaller decision than you had previously asked for.

Examples of things you could add with a Columbo moment include...

EXAMPLES

Asking them to sample a product.

Asking them to commit to a small order.

Inviting them to an event.

Introducing them to someone you think they should know.

Asking them to do something for you.

Asking them a question that creates scarcity in your first offer.

Using these moments and the Magic Words "Just one more thing" keeps the conversation alive and can help you avoid leaving with nothing.

22
A Favor

Success in life and business is rarely achieved without the support of others. If you can do things that allow other people to help you achieve your goals, then the chances of you reaching them significantly increase.

I am sure you have had many scenarios in which you have longed for someone else to do something that makes your life a little easier, that opens a door for you or provides you with the information you need to make the progress you would like.

As we reach the end of this book, perhaps you could do me a small favor?

Think for a second about how you feel about me asking you that direct question, "Could you do me a small favor?" I am pretty sure that in that split-second moment, you thought that you may be reasonably open to helping me out.

This is a simple and powerful set of Magic Words that you can use to get somebody to agree to do just about anything before they even know what the thing is. The request of a favor almost always gains a unanimous agreement from the recipient, and the worst response possible is still a conditional yes, like, "Depends what it is."

Think of the things that you could ask people to do following their agreement to the favor you are asking of them. I am sure your mind is boggled by the dozens of things you could add to your list of wants and the people who could help you with them. In this book I want to illustrate how much can be done with a powerful change of words. We can explore the application of these Magic Words using the topic of referrals.

Growing a new customer base from your existing happy customers is a solid strategy for business growth, yet it is often not implemented at all. I believe that there are three main reasons people fail to ask others for referrals:

1   They are too lazy and cannot be bothered.
2   They do not know *when* to ask.
3   They do not know *how* to ask.

Let's first consider the first option. Mostly it would relate to the people who do not read books, attend training or take their personal development seriously. This clearly does not describe you, so I guess we should consider the other two reasons.

When it comes to the timing, there are literally dozens of moments that you can ask for a referral. If you take the time to consider all the examples of "good times," they will all have one thing in common—the other person is happy. When people are happy with what you have done for them, there are some simple words that nearly always feature: they express their happiness with the words "Thank you." These words can easily trigger feelings of pride and self-worth in you. In addition to these feelings, then, it is important for you to understand the simplest reason why people say thank you.

An expression of gratitude comes from a feeling of indebtedness. Put simply, when they say thank you, it is because they feel they owe you something. The best time to ask for someone's help is when they feel indebted to you. All this means is, the next time you hear the words "Thank you" from your customer or prospect, use that as your cue to ask for more.

Now that you have the timing, let's next determine how to ask.

So, they have said, "Thank you," which provides you with your cue to ask your first question: "You couldn't do me a small favor, could you?" This simple question gains an almost certain agreeable response and gives you instant permission to continue with the rest of your request. You can then go on to say,

"You wouldn't happen to know…"

(This throws down a challenge, which makes people want to prove you wrong.)

"… just one person…"

(Just one, because it's reasonable and seems a simple ask, and they're more likely to think of someone by name.)

"… someone who, just like you…"

(This has the person narrowing down the options and gives you more of the right prospects, plus it pays a subtle compliment.)

"… would benefit from…"

And then emphasize the specific benefit or positive experience they have just thanked you for.

Then… *shut up!*

People say thank you when they feel they owe you something. **This is the best time to ask for someone's help.**

When they have thought of somebody, you need to know where to go next. You will probably see in their body language when they have thought of somebody. At this point, say, "Don't worry. I'm not looking for their details right now, but who was it that you were thinking of?"

This automatically takes the pressure off, and the "but" helps them to recall only the final part of the sentence. Find out then when they're next likely to see the person they thought of.

"You couldn't do me a further favor, could you? (I mean, they said yes the first time.) Next time you see Steve, could you share with him a little bit about how it was doing business with me and see if he's perhaps open-minded about taking a phone call from me to see if I can help him in the same way I helped you?"

Your prospect will almost certainly agree.

"Would it be okay if I gave you a call next week to find out how the chat with Steve went?"

They will most likely, again, be agreeable. You will then call when you said you would and ask, "I'm guessing you didn't get around to speaking to Steve?"

As a person of their word, either they will proudly say that they have spoken to Steve, or they will be embarrassed and tell you how they will go on to complete the introduction.

The magic in this, the crazy irony, is that you slow the process down, but you speed up the outcome and end up having conversations with people who expect your call, look forward to hearing from you and are grateful. It provides you with qualified future customers who already have third-party experience with your offerings, as well as permission to make contact. I would take that over a name and number any day of the week.

It is now time to do yourself a favor and look at all the things you can be asking of others, gaining their commitment before they even know what that thing is.

23

Just Out of Curiosity

There is one objection that people give in response to ideas that has always frustrated me. This objection is, "I just need some time to think about it."

I am not saying that people should feel rushed into decisions. It's just that my experience tells me this statement rarely means they are heading away to do a detailed analysis of their decision. They are just pushing their decision away to another day.

Apply some context to this, and consider that you have spent time responding to an inquiry, visiting a prospect, getting to know them and listening to their challenges. You then provide them with a detailed set of recommendations as to how you can help them achieve their objectives or overcome their challenges, and in return they provide this vague response that helps none in the discussion to reach closure.

My concern is that it is just not fair. I believe that if you have delivered your part correctly, then the other person at least owes you a little more transparency regarding their thoughts.

On receipt of this reply, I have often found myself wanting to shout, "What is it that you want to think about?" I knew that if they could open up their thoughts to me, then I could probably help. The trouble was, I knew I couldn't really ask that because it would seem rude or obnoxious. So instead, I hear people in my situation say things like, "It's okay, no pressure; we are ready when you are ready," and walk away from the opportunity hoping that time will fix it.

This frustration has meant that I have had to find a way of getting a real answer from people by asking rude, obnoxious questions without sounding rude or obnoxious. What I want from their response is not a guaranteed commitment, but honesty in the discussion so that we both know what the true obstacles are.

What I discovered was that if I preface one of these direct questions with a certain set of Magic Words, then I could change rude and obnoxious into soft and fluffy. By finding a reason for my direct question and gaining permission to ask it, I instantly shift control of the conversation to me. The words I use to do this are, "Just out of curiosity," and they can be used as the perfect preface to many a direct question.

Examples include… **EXAMPLES**

Just out of curiosity, what is it specifically you need some time to think about?

....

Just out of curiosity, what needs to happen for you to make a decision about this?

....

Just out of curiosity, what is it that's stopping you from moving forward with this right now?

....

In each of these examples, what is imperative is that you remain quiet following your question. Silence becomes your friend; you must not prejudge their answer or put words in their mouth. They now know they need to give you a proper answer, and one of two things will happen.

Asking big, brave questions is exactly what you need to do to become a professional mind-maker-upper.

Thing number one is that maybe twelve seconds goes by. (This will feel like three weeks.) They will then come back with a real, honest answer, and you can work with that transparency. The second option would be that the time runs on longer. This is good news. Bite your tongue, sit on your hands, do nothing. Let the time go by. During this elongated pause they are hunting for an excuse and often realize they do not really have one. They then respond with things like, "You know what, you're right. There isn't anything to think about," or, "There is nothing that needs to happen," or, "There is nothing stopping me." It's the very fact that you were prepared to ask them the question they were not yet prepared to ask themselves that empowers them to make a decision you both know was right for them in the first place. Asking big, brave questions is exactly what you need to do to move from being just like everybody else to becoming a professional mind-maker-upper.

Final Thought

With all these words to consider, I am sure you are now aware that reaching for the right words at the right time can make all the difference. There is one more thing I want to share with you, something that isn't necessarily a magic word.

It is something, though, that can make a huge and profound difference to your level of success when you impart your knowledge and wisdom to others.

One worry I hear from lots of people is the fear of being caught out when it comes to product knowledge about their business and industry and the need to have fantastic answers for every question.

About a decade ago I met one of the most successful salespeople I have ever known. I was having a conversation with him about success. This particular individual, Roger, was in the room when the very first text message was created, and he had had a long, illustrious career in the telecommunications industry. I remember talking to him about the change in telephones moving from analogue to digital, and he told me that he used to get questions from his customers all the time about how this new technology worked.

The question resulted in him trying to explain the technological updates and dazzle them with his deep knowledge—only to be greeted by blank faces looking back at him. In one of those light bulb moments that change everything, Roger realized he was doing everything wrong. He thought his obligation was to actually tell them how this stuff worked. He quickly realized his responsibility was not to give them *the* answer; it was just to give them *an* answer, so he changed the way he answered the question. From that point onward, when customers asked him, "So, how does all this stuff work?" he would respond with the words, "It works great." Nine times out of ten, his customers were delighted with that answer.

Think how that could work for you. When a customer or prospect asks how all this stuff works, could you just answer, "Great"? When they ask you what kind of results they could expect from this, could you answer, "Good ones"? By giving an answer that is simple, that is effortless, that is positive and uplifting, that comes back at them in the other direction, watch how it stuns people into a positive decision and empowers them to move forward, as opposed to confusing them with facts.

Give an answer that is simple, effortless, positive and uplifting, and watch how it stuns people into a positive decision.

Everything you have learned in this book is simple, is easy to do and, better still, works.

Everything you have learned in this book is simple, is easy to do and, better still, works.

What it does not do, though, is work with *all* of the people *all* of the time. It just works with *most* of the people *most* of the time. There is a chance that what you are doing now is working with *some* of the people *some* of the time, so please do not try this once and tell me it did not work. Try it over and over again until it becomes natural. Bring it into everyday language, and the compound effect of those tiny improvements and subtle changes in language, the ability to know exactly what to say and the insertion of a few Magic Words, could be just the tonic that takes your ambition, dedication and drive—with a few skills sprinkled on—and moves you from counting conversations to making conversations count.

I wish you all the success that you are prepared to work for. Please enjoy the journey.

Acknowledgements

In a life blessed with so many great people appearing in it, the idea of writing the acknowledgements for this book fills me with fear. Of course I will forget someone awesome, and no doubt there are hundreds of contributors who have influenced me without either of us even knowing it. I do know, though, that this book has only become a reality because of a handful of magical people.

The first thank-you, though, must go to the thousands of consumers who have given me a hard time over the years and have forced me to work on my craft and challenge myself to gain the experience to write this book. You cannot learn the power of simplicity until you have tackled the complications of reality. People often talk about how tricky sales people can be. My experience is that customers are no angels either!

Another huge thanks has to go to my first mentor, Peter Lee at instil (www.instil.co.uk), who, although I have thanked him in each of my books, still fails to realize the pure inspiration he provided to me when he showed me how much of a difference just one training session could make to someone's life.

My audiences from countless speaking gigs deserve a special mention. The hundreds of comments shared over the years have given me the fuel to document these words and archive something that I hope provides clarity to the tongue-tied tribe who are tenaciously trying to be triumphant.

More recently, I have to mention the amazing talents of Bob Burg, Scott Stratten and the community of professional speakers who spill their experience freely and remind me how inferior I am on a daily basis!

The book itself has only been made possible through a powerful collaboration with the special team of people at Page Two Strategies. In particular I want to call out Trena White for being a sensible voice of reason when I nearly decided not to finish the book, Gabrielle Narsted for keeping everything on track and making me feel like a naughty schoolboy if I missed a deadline and the ever-patient Jenny Govier, whose editing talent ensures you would never know that I can only write "British" and clearly never went to college!

Finally, it is often said that behind every great man is a great women. In my case this is amplified by the thanks that I owe to two great women. Firstly is my dedicated and loyal assistant Bonnie Schaefer, who effortlessly has my back in every scenario, is always one step ahead and allows me to do the things that I do best. There is one thank-you that always leaves me lost for words, and that is to my beautiful wife, Charlotte, for whom I would need to write another book to show my true gratitude. It is her presence that challenges me to be better in all that I do, and the fact that I closed the deal on her gives me all the confidence I need that these Magic Words really do work! Thank you for everything.

About the Author

Writing about yourself is the worst. How do I share my experience without sounding braggy? Do you really care that much anyway? Should I just write it in third person and see how that sounds?

These are all the questions I find myself struggling with as I write this. Yes, I have enjoyed a challenging and varied career, and I have achieved a lot through failing miserably and learning fast. It's true, I do live pretty much the life of my dreams (I drive the car I had a poster of on my bedroom wall as a kid and have two homes in the locations I added to dream boards in my teens) and people do say nice things about me and the results I have helped them achieve. The reality is, though, that I am just a normal guy who is the son of a builder and who is doing the best he can to make rhyme or reason of this crazy world we live in.

My passions are my health, people and the belief that one person can change the world. I am on a mission to change the way people think about selling and to help them realize that "sales" is not a dirty word. You can catch up with me on my mission of #teachingtheworldtosell on all the popular social channels. I would love to learn about your successes with the #magicwords.

Remember that contacts are in contact with each other, so let's please continue the conversation.

See my random pictures on Instagram: @philmjonesuk

Read automated posts and impromptu rants on Twitter: @philmjonesuk

Connect for business chatter on LinkedIn: https://www.linkedin.com/in/philmjones/

Gain free training resources on my Facebook page: www.facebook.com/philmjonessales

One more thing . . .
Check out my website: www.philmjones.com for my blog and some more cool stuff.

A Shameless Plug

My guess is that if you have got this far in the book, then you must have enjoyed it at least a little bit. Modern books are now judged using the universal recognition of an Amazon review. I'm not sure if it's for you, but would it be okay for you to take a few seconds and help me win a bet with a speaker friend of mine that I can get more reviews than she does?

While I'm asking, I guess it would make sense to let you know how else we might be able to help each other.

Because I am smart enough to own all my publishing rights, my team and I can help you directly with bulk orders of this book and save you a fortune. We can also change the cover to suit your brand and may even be open to changing the examples to suit your specific industry. This customization is a service I perform for my speaking clients, and I would love the opportunity to discuss doing the same for you. Please email Bonnie at speaking@philmjones.com and we can set up a time to chat.

CPSIA information can be obtained
at www.ICGtesting.com
Printed in the USA
FFOW03n0848050218
44896630-45101FF